# CHILDREN'S
# ALL-STAR
# COOK BOOK

The royalties from the sales of this book will be used to buy extra educational and games equipment, which will benefit the pupils of Battle Hill First School in Wallsend, North Tyneside.

As Headmaster, I would therefore like to say a big 'thank you' to the celebrities whose favourite recipes have made this book possible, and also to yourselves for purchasing it.

Happy eating!

*David Scott*

# CHILDREN'S ALL-STAR COOK BOOK

**COMPILED BY DAVID SCOTT**

**COOKERY EDITOR: SUE JOHN**

*Illustrations by Clare Harrison*

**DRAGON**
Granada Publishing

Dragon Books
Granada Publishing Ltd
8 Grafton Street, London W1X 3LA

Published by Dragon Books 1984

First published by Blackie and Son Limited, 1983

Text copyright © Sue John 1983
Illustrations copyright © Clare Harrison 1983

ISBN 0-583-30732-9

Reproduced, printed and bound in Great Britain by
Hazell Watson & Viney Limited,
Aylesbury, Bucks

Set in Times

All rights reserved. No part of this publication may
be reproduced, stored in a retrieval system, or
transmitted, in any form, or by any means, electronic,
mechanical, photocopying, recording or otherwise,
without the prior permission of the publishers.

This book is sold subject to the conditions that it
shall not, by way of trade or otherwise, be lent,
re-sold, hired out or otherwise circulated
without the publisher's prior consent in any
form of binding or cover other than that in
which it is published and without a similar
condition including this condition being imposed
on the subsequent purchaser.

*Acknowledgements*
The publishers gratefully acknowledge permission to reprint copyright photographs as follows:

BBC Ronnie Corbett, Roy Castle, John Cleese, Tony Hart, Blue Peter team, David Jensen, Peter Davison, Colin Baker, Bob Wilson
EMI Cliff Richard
CLI Her Royal Highness, The Princess of Wales
Hamish Hamilton Mike Read, photograph by Beverley Lebarrow

The publishers have made every effort to trace copyright holders. If we have inadvertently omitted to acknowledge anyone we should be most grateful if this would be brought to our attention for correction at the first opportunity.

# CONTENTS

## MAIN DISHES

| | |
|---|---|
| Ronnie Corbett | Miniburgers  15 |
| Little and Large | Syd's Shrimps  17 |
| David Hamilton | Radio 1 Moussaka  18 |
| Magnus Pyke | E-N-O-R-M-O-U-S Kedgeree  20 |
| Benny Hill | Nice Salad  21 |
| Mike Read | Chilli Con Carne  22 |
| Simon Groom | Courgettes Blue Peter  23 |
| Roger Moore | 007 Spuds  24 |
| Mike Yarwood | VIP Meat Loaf  25 |
| Pam Ayres | Cotswold Fandango  26 |
| Colin Baker | Jansson's Temptation  27 |
| Tony Hart | Morph's Spinach  28 |
| Les Dawson | Mother-in-Law's Supper Dish  29 |
| Ian Botham | Botham's Bolognese 'Owzat  30 |
| Cannon and Ball | Funny Fish  31 |
| George Cole | Minder's Stuffed Peppers  33 |
| Gareth Edwards | Scrum Soup  35 |
| Rolf Harris | Didgeridoo Tandoori  37 |
| Su Pollard | Hi-De-Hi Salad  38 |
| Bobby Robson | Steak and Kidney Pudding  39 |
| Eric Morecambe | Eric's Lancashire Hot Pot  41 |
| Maggie Philbin | Super Store Special  42 |
| The Goodies | Baked Potato Starter  44 |
| Robert Robinson | Compere's Carbonara  45 |
| Peter Davison | Gammon Dr Who  46 |
| Cliff Richard | Beef Curry  47 |

## SNACKS

| | |
|---|---|
| David Bellamy | Welsh Rarebit 48 |
| Gordon Jackson | The Professional Crumpet 49 |
| David Yip | Yip's Dip 50 |
| Una Stubbs | Home-made Muesli 51 |
| The Krankies | Potato Scones 52 |
| Patrick Moore | Star Snack 53 |
| Dickie Davies | Sportsman Sandwich 54 |
| Roy Castle | S'Mores Record Breakers 55 |
| HRH, The Princess of Wales | Royal Fudge 56 |

## DRINKS

| | |
|---|---|
| Christopher Timothy | Vet's Milkshake 57 |
| June Whitfield | June's Cooler 58 |
| Graeme Souness | Pop of the Kop 59 |
| Isla St Clair | Isla's Hot Chocolate and Clair's Cool Coffee 60 |

## CAKES AND BISCUITS

| | |
|---|---|
| Brigit Forsyth | Glamourjacks 61 |
| Bill Beaumont | Captain's Cake 62 |
| Tim Brooke-Taylor | Goody Goody Yum Yums 64 |
| Steve Ovett | Cut-and-Run Cake 65 |
| Bryan Mosley | Grocer's Goo Cake 66 |
| Hannah Gordon | Malt Loaf 67 |
| Barry Sheene | Just Amazing Coffee Cake 68 |
| Lawrie McMenemy | Manager's Majorcan Slice 69 |
| Stuart Hall | Knock-Out Krispies 70 |
| Floella Benjamin | Wally Cake 71 |
| Janet Brown | Brown's American Brownies 72 |
| Paul Daniels | Magic Biscuits 73 |

Paul & Linda
  McCartney                Wings Special    74

## PUDDINGS

Julia Williams         Angels' Orange Surprise    75
David Jensen           Kid's Mousse    76
Russ Abbot             Madhouse Gooseberry Tart    77
Todd Carty             Tucker's Apple Amber    78
Ian Ogilvy             Saint Sauce    79
Stephanie Turner       Bravo Macaroons    80
Paula Ann Bland        Grange Hill Gateau    81
Bob Wilson             Match of the Day Cheesecake    82
Ernie Wise             Wisecrack Crunch    84
Sarah Lam              Bread and Butter Pudding    85
Mick Robertson         Freetime Chocolate Bananas    86
Jon Pertwee            Worzel's Fresh Fruit Salad    87

## JUST FOR A LAUGH

Barry Cryer            Hard-Boiled Egg    88
Marti Caine            Beans on Toast    89
John Cleese            Ferret Supreme    90
Johnny Morris          Garden Peas    91
Kieran Prendiville     Lettuce    92
Chas and Dave          Stuffed Camel    93
Spike Milligan         Sweet Spaghetti    94

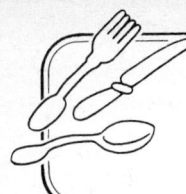

# OFF YOU GO

Before you cook, read right through the recipe and check that you have got the correct ingredients. Check that you have enough time to prepare and cook the dish.

Put on an apron and wash your hands before you start. Keep the kitchen as clean and tidy as possible while you work. Get out all the ingredients and equipment you will be needing.

Wash up as you go along and mop up any spilt food or liquids straightaway, to avoid slipping in the kitchen.

Take care when using sharp knives.

If you're not sure about a recipe ask an adult to help you.

Be extra careful when using the oven, grill or cooker top. Turn saucepan handles inwards – to avoid knocking them over accidentally.

Leave the kitchen clean and tidy – that means washing up and putting things away!

## COOKING HINTS

We could fill a whole book with cooking hints, but here are a few which you will find particularly useful when using this book.

When 'rubbing in' fat with the flour, use the fat straight from the refrigerator – it will be less sticky.

For 'creaming' or 'beating' use soft margarine or butter, which has been left at room temperature for an hour or two.

In recipes that use glacé cherries, rinse the cherries in a sieve under hot running water – this will make them easier to cut up.

When you measure spoonfuls of syrup, heat the spoon before you start by dipping it in a jug or bowl of boiling water.

Use scissors for snipping herbs or cutting bacon.

When you grease tins, take a knob of butter on a piece of kitchen paper. Rub the butter carefully into any corners and up the sides and base of the tin. Even non-stick tins need greasing.

## USING THE OVEN

Oven temperatures are given in each recipe. Light the oven before you start – this gives enough time for the oven to reach the correct temperature.

Always use oven gloves when putting food in or taking it out of the oven. Put hot dishes or tins on to a mat or board when first taking them from the oven.

Remember to turn the oven off when you have finished.

## MEASURING INGREDIENTS

You do not need kitchen scales to make the recipes in this book.

You can easily measure fats by cutting the correct amount from the block.

As a guide to measuring dry ingredients:

| | |
|---|---|
| 1 heaped tablespoon flour | = 25g |
| 1 level tablespoon white sugar | = 25g |
| 1 rounded tablespoon soft brown sugar | = 25g |

The number of people each dish will feed is given at the end of the recipe. If you want to alter the amount, remember to change the quantities before you start.

## PREPARATION OF VEGETABLES

### Potatoes
Put some cold water into the sink and put in the potatoes. If they are to be 'baked in their jackets', scrub them with a nail brush. Otherwise, use a potato peeler or a small sharp knife and remove as thin a layer of skin as possible. Wash them in the water while you are peeling. If you are not using the peeled potatoes straightaway put them in a clean bowl of cold water until you are ready for them.

### Carrots
These are prepared in the same way as potatoes – young carrots need scrubbing – old ones need peeling. Cut off each end with a small sharp knife.

### Celery
Break the celery into 'sticks' and put into cold water. Scrub each stick with a nail brush to remove the dirt. Cut off the root end and the leafy tops.

### Mushrooms
Never soak mushrooms. Wipe them with a piece of damp kitchen paper.

### Onions
By hand, peel off the outer papery skin. Using a sharp knife cut off the root and the top, if necessary. Rinse the onion under cold running water and wash your hands after handling them – do not rub your eyes!

### Leeks
Using a sharp knife cut off the roots and broken or torn green ends. Peel off the outer layer if it is very dirty or torn.

**Garlic**
Break off the number of cloves required and peel off the papery skin. Now place the garlic into a crusher to extract the juices for the recipe. If you do not have a garlic crusher, put the peeled cloves on to a small plate and crush with a table knife. Throw out the skin and use the juices which you have pressed out.

**Salad Ingredients and Fruit**
Never soak any fresh ingredients. Wash them as quickly and lightly as possible and shake dry any leaves (eg lettuce) immediately.

# MAIN DISHES

## RONNIE CORBETT
*Comedian*

### Miniburgers
**(Hamburgers with Cream Sauce)**

50g butter
1 medium onion – finely chopped
500g minced beef
1 level teaspoon salt
black pepper
1 egg
flour

a little oil
150ml beef stock – made from a stock cube
150ml single cream
pinch of nutmeg
a few green herbs – parsley, chives, tarragon

Put half the butter into a mixing bowl and soften with a wooden spoon. Add the chopped onion, minced beef and seasoning. Tap the middle of the egg shell on the edge of the bowl and let the egg drop into the bowl. Mix well with the wooden spoon.

Sprinkle a little flour on the worktop and on your hands. Take small handfuls of the mixture and shape into small hamburgers – about 6 cms across and 1.5 cms deep. (You should have about 20).

Put 1–2 tablespoons oil into a frying pan and put on a moderate heat. Using a slice, fry the hamburgers for about 4 minutes each side. Lift them on to a warmed serving dish and put them in a very low oven (Gas ½ – 250°F – 120°C).

Fry all the hamburgers. If there is any oil left in the frying pan carefully pour it into a small bowl.

Pour the stock into the frying pan and stir with the meat juices that are left in the pan. Boil the liquid for about 2 minutes until it has reduced and thickened. Add the cream and boil for 1 minute.

Meanwhile put the remaining butter on a small plate. Add nutmeg and using scissors snip in a few herbs (about 2 tablespoons). Using a palette knife soften the butter and herbs.

Remove the frying pan from the heat and, stirring with a tablespoon, mix in the butter, a small amount at a time. Pour the sauce over the hamburgers and serve straightaway.
*5–6 servings*

Serve with new potatoes and a fresh green vegetable.

# LITTLE AND LARGE
*Comedians*

*The following recipe is guaranteed to make Little people Larger.*

## Syd's Shrimps

3 tablespoons olive oil
1–2 cloves garlic, crushed
225g frozen prawns or shrimps
225g button mushrooms
50g butter
1 lemon
salt and pepper

Pour the oil into a frying pan and put over a moderate heat. Add the garlic and the shrimps. Fry for about 7 minutes, turning over occasionally with a slice.

Wipe the mushrooms with a piece of damp kitchen paper. Then slice them, using a small sharp knife. Melt the butter in another frying pan, and add the mushrooms. Fry for 1 minute.

Add the mushrooms to the shrimps. Cut the lemon in half and squeeze the juice over the shrimps. Season with a little salt and pepper. Turn the heat down to low and simmer gently for another 4–5 minutes. Serve straightaway.
*2–3 servings*

Delicious served with boiled rice or on toast.

# DAVID HAMILTON
*Disc Jockey*

## Radio 1 Moussaka

2 medium sized aubergines – washed
salt
vegetable oil
1 medium sized onion – peeled, sliced and chopped
500g minced beef
1 397g can tomatoes
2 tablespoons tomato purée
salt and pepper
125ml water
1 packet cheese sauce mix
300ml milk
50g strong Cheddar cheese – grated

Using a small sharp knife cut off the stalk end from the aubergines and then slice them across into .5 cm slices. Lay them out (on the sink board if possible) and sprinkle with salt. Leave for 10 minutes.

Put 2 tablespoons oil into a medium saucepan and put over a moderate heat. Add the onion and mince and fry for about 5 minutes, turning with a wooden spoon until the meat has browned. Add the tomatoes, purée, seasoning and water. Bring to the boil, stir, then cover and simmer for 20 minutes.

Wipe the salt from the aubergines with damp kitchen paper. Pour a little oil into a frying pan and put over a moderate heat. Using a slice, lay some aubergine slices in the pan. Fry for 2 minutes on each side. Lift the cooked aubergines on to a warm plate, until they are all cooked. (You may need to add more oil for frying).

Layer the meat and aubergines in an ovenproof dish, ending with the aubergines. Prepare the cheese sauce, using

the milk, as directed on the packet. Pour this over the aubergines and cover with the grated cheese. Bake in a moderately hot oven (Gas No. 5 – 375°F – 190°C) for 35–40 minutes until the top is golden brown.
*4 servings*

# MAGNUS PYKE
*TV Scientist*

### E-N-O-R-M-O-U-S **Kedgeree**

100g long grain rice
2 medium sized eggs
1 Finnan haddock

50g butter
cayenne pepper

Put the rice into a large saucepan, half full of boiling salted water. Stir once and boil for 15 minutes. Put the eggs into a small saucepan half full of cold water. Bring to the boil. Boil for 10 minutes. Put the haddock into a pan of boiling water and simmer gently for 10 minutes.

Drain the rice into a sieve or colander over the sink. Lift the eggs, with a spoon, from the boiling water. Using a slice lift the fish on to a board. Flakc the flesh from the skin and with a fork mix the flesh and butter together in a warmed bowl. Add the rice and a little pepper. Mix together. Carefully remove the shells from the eggs and slice with a small sharp knife. Arrange on top of the kedgeree and serve straightaway.
*3 servings*

# BENNY HILL
*Comedian*

## Nice Salad
**(Salade Niçoise)**

2 hard boiled eggs (see p 20, Kedgeree recipe)
1 397g can new potatoes
4 tomatoes – sliced
¼ cucumber – sliced
1 small onion – peeled, sliced and chopped
1 198g can tuna fish
1 50g can anchovy fillets
a few capers
a few black olives
small bunch parsley – chopped

**Vinaigrette dressing:**
8 tablespoons olive oil
3 tablespoons white wine vinegar
½ teaspoon salt
freshly ground black pepper
½ teaspoon french mustard

Prepare the hard boiled eggs, remove the shells and using a small sharp knife, cut the eggs into quarters. Drain the potatoes and cut into .5 cm slices.

Arrange the sliced tomatoes and cucumber on the bottom and sides of 4 individual salad bowls. Divide the sliced potatoes between the bowls and add a little of the chopped onion.

Place a quarter of the tuna fish in the middle of each salad and put 2 quarters of egg on either side. Make a crisscross pattern of anchovies on top. Add a few capers, olives and the remaining onion. Sprinkle a little parsley over the top.

To make the dressing, put all the ingredients into a small screwtop jar and shake vigorously for a minute.

Just before serving divide the dressing between the salads.

*4 servings*

# MIKE READ
*Disc Jockey*

## Chilli Con Carne

1 tablespoon oil
750g minced beef
1 large onion – peeled and finely chopped
1 green pepper – seeded and chopped
1 397g can tomatoes
salt and pepper
1–2 teaspoons chilli powder (add more or less according to how hot you like it)
1 tablespoon vinegar
1 teaspoon sugar
2 level tablespoons tomato purée
200ml water
1 425g can red kidney beans

Put the oil into a large saucepan and fry the mince and onion over a moderate heat until lightly browned. Add all the remaining ingredients except the kidney beans. Stir with a wooden spoon, cover and simmer over a very low heat for 30 minutes. Drain the liquid from the kidney beans and add them to the mince. Stir and cook for a further 10 minutes. **Serve straightaway.**
*4 servings*

Serve with a mixed side salad and some crusty bread.

# SIMON GROOM
*TV Presenter*

## Courgettes Blue Peter

25g butter
1 small onion – sliced and chopped
1 clove garlic – crushed
450g small courgettes
100g button mushrooms – wiped with damp kitchen paper
1 small tin tomatoes
1 level teaspoon dried basil
salt and pepper

Put the butter into a large frying pan and put over a moderate heat to melt. Add the onion and garlic. Shake the pan gently, put on the lid and fry for about 4 minutes.

Wash the courgettes. Using a small sharp knife, cut off both ends and then slice the courgettes into 1 cm thick slices. Add them and add the mushrooms to the pan. Shake gently, replace the lid and cook gently for 10 minutes.

Add the tomatoes and basil. Season well, replace lid and cook for a further 10 minutes, stirring from time to time. Serve straightaway.

*4 servings*

Try sprinkling grated cheese on the top when you serve it. This dish goes well with mashed potatoes and a green vegetable.

# ROGER MOORE
*Actor*

## 007 Spuds
**(Creamed Cheese Potatoes)**

900g potatoes – peeled and cut into 1 cm cubes
1 medium onion – sliced and chopped
25g flour
salt and pepper
small bunch of parsley – washed
100g Cheddar cheese – grated
150ml milk
150ml double cream

Put the cubed potatoes and chopped onion into a mixing bowl. Using a tablespoon, stir in the flour, salt and pepper. Using scissors snip the parsley finely into the bowl. Stir in half the grated cheese.

Take a knob of butter on a piece of kitchen paper and grease the inside of a 2 litre ovenproof dish. Put the potato mixture into the dish.

Warm the milk in a small saucepan. Remove from the heat and add the cream. Stir and pour over the potatoes. Sprinkle the remaining cheese on top and bake in a hot oven (Gas No. 6 – 400°F – 200°C) for 1¼–1½ hours. Serve straightaway.

*4–6 servings*

# MIKE YARWOOD
*Comedian*

## VIP Meat Loaf

1 medium egg
2 tablespoons milk
3 slices granary bread – crumbled
450g minced beef
1 medium onion – finely chopped
1 stick celery – finely chopped
a few mushrooms – finely chopped
2 rashers bacon
2 level tablespoons tomato purée
1 clove garlic – crushed
salt and pepper

Tap the middle of the egg shell on the edge of a mixing bowl and let the egg drop into the bowl. Beat the egg with a fork.

Add the milk and the breadcrumbs. Mix in the mince, onions, celery and mushrooms. Using scissors snip the lean bacon into the bowl and keep the fattier part on one side. Add the purée and garlic and season well.

Take a shallow oblong ovenproof dish. Using your hands shape the mixture in the dish into a loaf shape. Lay the fattier strips of bacon on the top. Bake in a moderate oven (Gas No. 4 – 350°F – 180°C) for 1½ hours. Serve straightaway or keep and serve cold.

*4 servings*

# PAM AYRES
*Poet*

## Cotswold Fandango

Oil
450g minced beef
1 medium onion – peeled, sliced and chopped
150ml beef stock – made from a stock cube
1 tablespoon tomato purée
salt and pepper
100g flour
1 egg
250ml milk

Put a little oil into a frying pan – just enough to cover the bottom. Put over a moderate heat and add the beef and onion. Using a slice, turn the meat over and fry for about 8 minutes until the meat is evenly browned. Add the stock, purée and seasonings. Cook for a further 5 minutes. Pour the meat and gravy into a large ovenproof dish.

Sieve the flour and ½ teaspoon salt into a mixing bowl. Tap the middle of the egg shell on the edge of the bowl and let the egg drop into the flour. Add a little milk and using a wooden spoon beat the batter mixture very hard. Slowly add all the milk, beating all the time. Pour the batter over the meat and bake in a hot oven (Gas No. 7 – 425°F – 220°C) for about an hour – until the top is golden brown. Serve straightaway.

*4 servings*

# COLIN BAKER
*Actor*

*I first tried this popular recipe in Sweden. It is very tasty and filling.*

## Jansson's Temptation

1 198g can tuna fish in oil
2 large onions – peeled and chopped
8 medium potatoes – peeled and sliced (.5cm thick)
salt and pepper
125ml single cream
50g breadcrumbs
25g butter

Take a knob of butter on a piece of kitchen paper and rub round the inside of an ovenproof dish. Drain the oil from the tuna and spread the fish on the bottom of the dish. Cover with the onions. Arrange the sliced potatoes on top and season well with the salt and pepper. Pour over the cream. Sprinkle the breadcrumbs on top. Cut the butter into small pieces and dot over the breadcrumbs. Bake in a hot oven (Gas No. 6 – 400°F – 200°C) for about 1 hour, until the potatoes are tender. Serve straightaway.
*4 servings*

# TONY HART
*Artist/TV Presenter*

## Morph's Spinach

450g spinach  
salt  
30g butter  
1 clove of garlic – crushed  
freshly ground black pepper

Tear the stalks from the spinach and put the leaves into a sink of cold water. Shake the leaves in the water to remove any dirt or grit. Put the leaves into a large saucepan and add 1 teaspoon of salt and 125ml cold water. Cover the pan with a lid and put over a moderate heat. Shake the pan occasionally and cook for 5–7 minutes, until the spinach is tender.

While this is cooking, put the butter on to a small plate and using a palette knife work in the crushed garlic and pepper. Drain the spinach into a colander, over the sink, shake well and tip into a small warmed serving dish. Top with the garlic butter and serve straightaway.

*3–4 servings*

# LES DAWSON
*Comedian*

## Mother-in-Law's Supper Dish

1 large potato
approx. 25g Cheddar cheese
  – grated
approx. 25g butter
basil

Scrub the potato but do not peel it. Using an apple corer remove some of the centre of the potato. Fill the hole with grated cheese, butter and a pinch of basil. Press well down. Take a square of aluminium foil and wrap the potato in it. Bake at the top of a moderately hot oven (Gas No. 5 – 375°F – 190°C) for 1–1¼ hours. Hold the potato in an oven glove to check if it is soft. Serve straightaway.
*Allow 1 potato for each person*

Delicious served with cabbage.

# IAN BOTHAM
*Cricketer*

## Botham's Bolognese 'Owzat
**(Spaghetti Bolognese)**

2 tablespoons oil
250g lean minced beef
1 medium onion – peeled, sliced and chopped
1 397g can tomatoes
2 tablespoons tomato purée
1 clove garlic – crushed
2 teaspoons sugar
salt and pepper
1 bay leaf
a little water
350g spaghetti
25g butter
Parmesan cheese

Put the oil into a medium sized saucepan and heat it over a moderate heat. Add the mince and the onion and fry for about 5 minutes, turning with a wooden spoon until the meat has browned.

Add the tomatoes, purée, garlic, sugar, seasoning and bay leaf. Bring to the boil, stir, then cover the pan and simmer gently for 40 minutes. You may need to add a little water during the cooking if the mixture looks dry.

After about 25 minutes, fill a large saucepan three-quarters full with water and bring to the boil. Add 1 teaspoon salt. Hold the spaghetti carefully in a bundle, then push it down into the boiling water. Stir it once and then boil it fast for about 12 minutes.

Tip the spaghetti into a colander over the sink and then tip it into a warm bowl. Add the butter and freshly ground black pepper. Toss around. Pour the meat sauce into a bowl and serve straightaway with the spaghetti. Serve with a small bowl of grated Parmesan cheese.

*4 servings*

# CANNON AND BALL
*Comedians*

## Funny Fish
**(Fish in White Sauce)**

450g cod or haddock fillet
salt and pepper
½ lemon
50g butter
600g potatoes – peeled and cut into even sized pieces
a little milk
1 packet cheese sauce mix
2 tomatoes – sliced

Wipe the fish with a piece of damp kitchen paper and lay them in a large shallow ovenproof dish. Season and squeeze the lemon juice over the fish. Taking half the butter, dot it over the fish. Cover the dish with aluminium foil and bake in a moderately hot oven (Gas No. 5 – 375°F – 190°C) for 25 minutes.

Meanwhile, half fill a large saucepan with water and bring to the boil. Add the potatoes and 1 teaspoon salt and boil until the potatoes are tender – 10–15 minutes. Drain them into a colander over the sink and then return them to the saucepan – but not over the heat. Add the remaining butter and about 3 tablespoons milk. Using a potato masher mash them until they are smooth.

When the fish is cooked spoon off the liquid into a measuring jug and make up to the quantity as given on the packet of cheese sauce mix, with milk. Use this fish and milk liquid to make up the cheese sauce as directed.

Put the mashed potato around the edge of the fish dish and fork it up lightly. Pour the sauce over the fish and lay the

sliced tomatoes down the centre of the dish. Return to the oven for 15 minutes to lightly brown the potato. Serve straightaway.
*4 servings*

If you have a piping bag and a large icing pipe you could pipe the mashed potato round the dish.

# GEORGE COLE
*Actor*

## Minder's Stuffed Peppers

4 medium sized green peppers
75g long grain rice
salt and pepper
2 tablespoons oil
350g minced beef
1 medium onion – peeled, sliced and chopped
100g mushrooms – wiped and sliced
1 teaspoon paprika
Worcester Sauce
50g Cheddar cheese – thinly sliced

Using a small sharp knife cut the tops off the peppers and remove the seeds from the inside. Put the peppers and the tops into a large saucepan, cover them with water, bring to the boil and simmer for 3 minutes. Drain them into a colander over the sink.

Half fill a medium sized saucepan with water and bring to the boil. Add the rice and 1 teaspoon salt, stir and boil for 8 minutes. Drain through a colander or sieve over the sink.

Put the oil into a medium sized saucepan and put over a moderate heat. Add the mince and the chopped onions. Fry for 5 minutes, turning the meat with a wooden spoon, until it is browned. Add the mushrooms and the cooked rice and simmer gently for about 10 minutes. Add the paprika, salt and pepper and a few drops of Worcester Sauce and stir round.

Stand the peppers upright in an ovenproof dish and divide the meat mixture between them. Any extra meat can be put in the dish around the peppers. Add 4 tablespoons water to the dish and replace the pepper 'lids'. Arrange the sliced

cheese over the tops and bake in a moderately hot oven (Gas No. 5 – 375°F – 190°C) for 40 minutes. Serve straightaway.
*4 servings*

If you're courting or over 40 double the Paprika!

# GARETH EDWARDS
*Ex Welsh International Rugby Player*

## Scrum Soup
**(Carrot Soup)**

450g carrots
1 medium onion – sliced
2 sticks celery – sliced
½ turnip or swede – peeled and sliced
25g butter
a few bacon rinds
750ml stock – made from a mixture of beef and chicken stock cubes
1 blade mace
1 bay leaf
a few herbs – parsley or thyme
1 level tablespoon cornflour
250ml milk
salt and pepper

Scrub the carrots if they are young, or peel them – with a potato peeler – if they are old. Using a small sharp knife cut off the tops. Cut them into 1 cm thick slices. Prepare the other vegetables.

Melt the butter with the bacon rinds in a large saucepan over a low heat. Add all the prepared vegetables, shake the pan, cover with a lid and cook over a low heat for 4–5 minutes.

Add the stock, mace, bay leaf and a few other herbs. Stir with a wooden spoon, replace the lid and simmer gently for 20–30 minutes until the vegetables are tender.

Place a sieve over a mixing bowl and pour the soup into the sieve. Using a wooden spoon press the vegetables through the sieve. Mix the cornflour and milk together in a small bowl. Pour the puréed soup back into the saucepan

and using a wooden spoon stir in the cornflour mixture. Add salt and pepper and cook for 5 more minutes. If the soup is too thick add a little more milk or water.
*4 servings*

# ROLF HARRIS
*Artist/Entertainer*

## Didgeridoo Tandoori
**(Tandoori Chicken)**

4 chicken pieces
1 453g carton natural yoghurt
1 64g can tomato purée
about 25g fresh ginger – grated
grated rind of 1 lemon
1 teaspoon paprika
4 bay leaves – crumbled
6 whole peppercorns
1 teaspoon chilli powder
salt and pepper
4–6 cloves of garlic – crushed

Wipe the chicken with a piece of damp kitchen paper. Using a sharp knife make 2 or 3 cuts across the flesh of each chicken piece.

Put all the other ingredients into a large mixing bowl and stir with a tablespoon. Add the chicken and cover with the mixture. Cover the bowl with aluminium foil and leave overnight.

Next day, line a roasting tin with foil and put a rack (use the grill pan rack) in the tin. Place the chicken pieces on the rack and spoon all the mixture over them. Bake in a moderately hot oven (Gas No. 5 – 375°F – 190°C) for about 1–1½ hours, until the chicken is tender and crispy on the top. Serve straightaway with a bowl of rice and a salad.
*4 servings*

Yoghurt with cucumber and onions is a good cooling sauce if you have been heavy handed with the chilli powder!

# SU POLLARD
*Actress*

*This dish gives me as much pleasure as Roast Duckling.*

## Hi-De-Hi Salad
**(Greek Salad)**

1 small or ½ large lettuce – washed and shaken dry
2 tomatoes – washed and quartered
½ cucumber
1 small onion – peeled and thinly sliced
6 black olives
100g packet fetta cheese
3 tablespoons olive oil
1 tablespoon white vinegar
salt and pepper

Using your hands tear the lettuce leaves into small pieces. Put them into a salad bowl and add the quartered tomatoes.

Wash the cucumber and using a small, sharp knife cut off the end. Cut the cucumber in half and then into half again, lengthways. Cut these lengths of cucumber into dice and add to the bowl.

By hand, carefully push the sliced onion into rings and add to the bowl with the olives.

Open the cheese and with a small, sharp knife cut the cheese into approximately 2 cm cubes and add to the salad. Add the oil, vinegar, salt and pepper. Using a tablespoon and a fork, gently toss the salad in the bowl until it is well mixed.

*4 servings*

This can be eaten on its own or with nice big chips!

# BOBBY ROBSON
*England Manager*

## Steak and Kidney Pudding

**Suet Pastry:**
200g self raising flour
pinch of salt
100g shredded beef suet
8 tablespoons water

500g stewing steak
50g ox kidney

1 tablespoon flour
salt and pepper
1 onion – peeled and chopped
a little water

To make the pastry, sieve the flour and salt into a mixing bowl. Add the suet and mix together with your finger tips. Add the water and using a palette knife stir round to form a dough.

Take a little butter on a piece of kitchen paper and rub round the inside of a 1 litre china pudding basin. Sprinkle a little flour on the worktop and rolling pin. Take two thirds of the pastry and roll it into a circle – large enough to line the pudding basin.

Wipe the meat with a piece of damp kitchen paper and using a large sharp knife cut the steak and kidney into approximately 2 cm cubes. Put the flour, salt and pepper on to a plate and toss the meat in it.

Put some of the meat into the pastry-lined basin, then a layer of onion. Repeat this using all the meat and onion. Pour about 3 tablespoons water over the meat and damp the top edge of the pastry. Roll out the remaining pastry to a circle to fit the top of the pudding. Lift on to the pudding and press the edges well together.

Take a piece of aluminium foil about 30 cm square and rub a little butter over one side. Make a pleat down the centre of the foil and place buttered side down over the pudding. Tuck the foil carefully over the edge of the basin.

Prepare the steamer* and when the water is bubbling gently put the basin into the top of the steamer. Steam for 4 hours – check every half hour to see if you need to add more water. Serve in the basin, straightaway.
*4 servings*

*Ask an adult to set up the steamer for you and to be around during the cooking time.

# ERIC MORECAMBE
*Comedian*

## Eric's Lancashire Hot Pot

4 best end neck of lamb cutlets
450g potatoes – peeled and thinly sliced
2 medium onions – peeled and sliced
salt and pepper
150ml water
25g butter or margarine

Wipe the cutlets with a piece of damp kitchen paper. Cover the base of a 1 litre ovenproof casserole with a layer of potatoes. Add the onions and cutlets. Season well. Arrange the remaining potatoes in an attractive overlapping pattern on the top. Pour in the water. Cut the butter into small pieces and dot over the top. Cover with a lid or aluminium foil and bake in a moderate oven (Gas No. 4 – 350°F – 180°C) for 1½ hours. Remove the lid and cook for another half hour to lightly brown the potato topping. Serve straight-away.

*4 servings*

# MAGGIE PHILBIN
*TV Presenter*

*This dish is really quick to cook, so it's the one I cook when I get back from a busy day.*

## Super Store Special

Selection of washed vegetables, such as cauliflower, leeks, onions, potatoes, peppers – weighing about 1kg in total

**Cheese Sauce:**
50g butter or margarine
50g flour
600ml milk
salt and pepper
100g Cheddar cheese – grated
pinch of cayenne pepper
pinch of mustard powder

Prepare the vegetables: break the cauliflower into florets, slice the cleaned leeks into 1cm thick slices, peel and quarter the onions, peel and cut the potatoes into 2 cm cubes and cut the pepper (after removing the seeds) into 2 cm squares.

Quarter fill a medium saucepan with water and bring to the boil. Add 1 teaspoon salt and add the potatoes and onions. Boil for 5 minutes and add the leeks for a further 3 minutes. In a separate saucepan boil the cauliflower for about 6 minutes. The vegetables should be just tender – do not overcook. The peppers do not need boiling. Drain the vegetables into a colander over the sink, add the peppers and put into a shallow ovenproof dish.

To make the sauce, melt the butter in a medium sized saucepan over a moderate heat, add the flour and stir with a wooden spoon. Add the milk slowly, beating all the time.

The sauce should be smooth and shiny after cooking for 2 minutes.

Remove from the heat, add the cheese and seasonings. Pour the sauce over the vegetables and bake in a hot oven (Gas No. 7 – 425°F – 220°C) for about 25 minutes until the top is golden brown. Serve straightaway.

*4 servings*

You could add any left-over cooked vegetables such as carrots, peas or crisp cabbage.

# THE GOODIES
*Comedians*

## Baked Potato Starter

even sized potatoes
sour cream
a small bunch of chives
black lumpfish roe
lemon quarters

For each person, scrub one potato. Put the potato on a board, and using a small sharp knife push the knife deep into the potato in 4 places. Bake in a moderately hot oven (Gas No. 5 – 375°F – 190°C) for 1–1½ hours.

To test when the potato is cooked through, hold it in an oven glove and press gently – it should be soft. Put the potato on a warm plate and cut a cross on the top with a small sharp knife.

Fill with a tablespoonful of sour cream and using scissors snip a few chives over the cream. Add a tablespoonful of lumpfish roe and serve straightaway with quarters of lemon.

# ROBERT ROBINSON
*TV Presenter*

## Compere's Carbonara
**(Spaghetti alla Carbonara)**

salt
225g spaghetti
6 rashers streaky bacon
25g butter

2 medium eggs
2 tablespoons double cream
freshly ground black pepper
Parmesan cheese

Three quarters fill a large saucepan with water and bring to the boil. Add 1 teaspoon salt, and holding the spaghetti in a bundle gently lower it into the fast boiling water. Stir with a long handled spoon or fork and then let it boil for 10–12 minutes.

Meanwhile, using scissors, snip the bacon finely. Melt the butter over a low heat in a frying pan and add the bacon. Cook slowly for 5 minutes, shaking the pan from time to time.

Tap the middle of the egg shell on the edge of a small bowl and carefully let the egg drop into the bowl. Repeat with the other egg and whisk them with a fork. Add the cream and some black pepper.

When the spaghetti is cooked tip it carefully into a colander over the sink. Return the spaghetti to the pan and add the bacon and butter. Using a fork toss the spaghetti round for 1 minute. Now add the cream and egg mixture and quickly toss it around until all the spaghetti has been coated with the sauce. Serve straightaway with a bowl of grated parmesan cheese to sprinkle over it.

*2 servings*

# PETER DAVISON
*Actor*

## Gammon Dr Who
**(Gammon Steak Hawaii)**

50g butter
50g soft brown sugar
3 tablespoons red wine
 vinegar
4 × 1 cm thick smoked
 gammon or bacon steaks
2 bananas
watercress

Put the butter, sugar and vinegar into a large frying pan and put it over a low heat until the sugar has dissolved and the butter melted, stirring with a slice. Add the steaks to the pan and cook gently for 4–5 minutes on each side.

Meanwhile peel the bananas and using a small sharp knife cut them into 2 cm thick slices. Using a slice lift the steaks from the pan on to a warm serving dish and keep warm in a very low oven.

Add the bananas to the pan and cook for 2 minutes, turning over with the slice. Add the bananas to the steak and any remaining sauce from the pan.

Arrange watercress around the dish and serve straightaway.

*4 servings*

# CLIFF RICHARD
*Singer*

## Beef Curry

450g braising steak
2 tablespoons oil
1 medium onion – sliced
3–4 level teaspoons curry powder – depending on how spicy you like curry
salt and pepper
½ teaspoon chilli powder
½ teaspoon ginger
1 level tablespoon tomato purée
1 clove garlic – crushed
300ml water
1 rounded teaspoon cornflour
150ml milk

Wipe the steak with a piece of damp kitchen paper and, using a large sharp knife, cut the meat into cubes and cut off any gristle or fat. Put the oil into a medium-sized saucepan and put over a moderate heat. Add the meat and the sliced onion and fry until the meat is lightly browned. Stir the meat with a wooden spoon to prevent it from sticking.

Add the curry, seasonings, chilli, ginger, purée, garlic and water. Stir and then cover the pan with a lid, turn the heat down as low as possible and simmer for 1½–2 hours until the meat is tender. Stir the curry from time to time and add a little more water if it seems to be drying up.

Mix the cornflour and milk together with a teaspoon in a small bowl and add to the curry. Stir and cook gently for a further ten minutes. Serve straightaway.
*3–4 servings*

Serve beef curry with plain boiled rice and popadams.

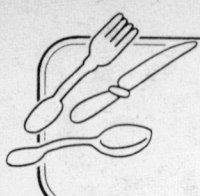

# SNACKS

## DAVID BELLAMY
*Botanist*

### Welsh Rarebit

1 slice of bread
butter to spread
about 30g Cheddar cheese – grated
1 egg

Light the grill at its highest and toast one side of the bread. Put the toast on a board and butter the untoasted side. Generously cover with grated cheese and put back under the grill until the cheese is golden brown.

Meanwhile, half fill a small frying pan with water and bring to the boil. Turn down the heat so the water is just bubbling. Carefully tap the middle of the egg on the edge of a cup and let the egg drop into it. Gently tip the egg into the bubbling water and 'poach' it for about 2 minutes. Using a slice, lift the egg from the water and serve it straightaway on top of the toasted cheese.

*1 serving*

# GORDON JACKSON
*Actor*

*A perfect snack! Not very exotic but kids love it.*

## The Professional Crumpet
### (Piping Hot Buttered Crumpets)

crumpets
butter for spreading
Marmite or Bovril

poached eggs – as described in Welsh Rarebit on page 48

Light the grill to its highest. Toast the underside of the crumpets for a minute, turn them over and toast the other side for another minute. Put on to plates, spread with butter and Marmite. Meanwhile have the eggs poaching. Using a slice lift an egg on to each crumpet. Serve straightaway.
*Allow 1 crumpet for each person*

# DAVID YIP
*Actor*

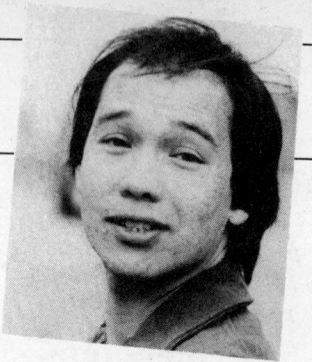

*I love to eat, but I try to take a sensible approach to it. My eating revolves mainly around vegetarian dishes...*

## Yip's Dip
### (Avocado Dip)

2–3 Avocado pears
juice of 1 lemon
1–2 tablespoons olive oil
salt and freshly ground black pepper
pitta bread

Using a small sharp knife cut the pears in half lengthways and take out the stones. Using a teaspoon scoop out all the flesh and put it into a blender or bowl. Add the lemon juice, oil and seasoning. Either liquidize for a few seconds in the blender or mash the pears with a fork. Check the dip for seasoning and add a little more oil, salt and pepper if you like.

Put the dip into a small serving bowl and serve straightaway with warm pitta bread to dip into it. Brown wholewheat bread is also good for dipping.

This would be nice to serve at a party.

# UNA STUBBS
*Actress*

## Home-made Muesli

1 teacup rolled oats
1 teacup milk
1 dessertspoon honey
1 handful sultanas
1 eating apple – washed and grated
1 banana – sliced

choice of extras – yoghurt, cream, nuts, dried apricots etc.

Put the oats into a bowl. Boil the milk in a small saucepan and pour it over the oats. Add the honey and sultanas and stir together. Cover the bowl and leave overnight. In the morning stir in the grated apple, sliced banana and any of the extras you like.
*2–3 servings*

# THE KRANKIES
*Comedy Duo*

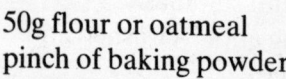

*I'm sure all other schoolboys will like my favourite food – Jimmy Krankie*

## Potato Scones

250g potatoes – peeled  
salt  
about 50g butter  
50g flour or oatmeal  
pinch of baking powder

Using a sharp knife cut the potatoes into even-sized pieces. Half fill a medium sized saucepan with water and bring to the boil. Add the potatoes and a little salt, cover and boil for about 10–15 minutes until they are tender.

Drain the potatoes into a colander over the sink and then tip them back into the saucepan. Add nearly half the butter and mash the potatoes with a potato masher. Add the flour and baking powder a bit at a time and work into the potatoes. Add ½ teaspoon salt.

Sprinkle a little extra flour on to the table and tip the potato mixture on to it. Using your hands shape it into a fat sausage – about 20 cms long. Using a sharp knife cut the mixture into 12 even slices.

Melt a little of the butter in a large frying pan and fry the scones over a moderate heat for 3–4 minutes on each side. Add a little more butter to fry the next batch. Keep them in a clean folded tea towel and eat while they are just warm.  
*12 scones*

You can cook them on a griddle if you have one.

# PATRICK MOORE
*Astronomer*

## Star Snack
(Selsey Rarebit)

1 slice bread
butter to spread
a few rings green or red pepper
about 30g Cheddar cheese – thinly sliced

Light the grill to its highest and toast the bread on one side only. Put the toast on to a board and butter the untoasted side. Lay a few pepper rings on the toast and cover with the slices of cheese. Put back under the grill until golden brown. Serve straightaway.
*1 serving*

Two of these Selsey Rarebits clapped together make one Martian pancake! PM

# DICKIE DAVIES
*TV Sports Presenter*

## Sportsman Sandwich
**(Bacon, Lettuce and Tomato Sandwich)**

8 rashers back bacon
6 slices bread
about 3 tablespoons
   mayonnaise

4 lettuce leaves – washed
4 medium tomatoes –
   washed and thinly sliced
salt and pepper

Using scissors, remove the rind from the bacon. Grill for 2–3 minutes on each side until crisp. Toast each side of the bread.

Put the toast on to a board and spread one side of each slice with mayonnaise. Arrange two rashers of bacon on 1 slice. Repeat with one other slice of toast. Cover each with a lettuce leaf and a few slices of tomato. Season with salt and pepper.

Cover with another slice of toast and add the remaining bacon, lettuce and tomatoes. Season and top with the last slice of toast (mayonnaise-side down!). Lightly press down the sandwiches and using a bread knife, cut each one in half diagonally. Serve straightaway.
*2 sandwiches*

# ROY CASTLE
*Entertainer*

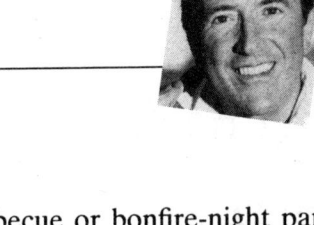

## S'Mores Record Breakers

Here is a tasty idea for a barbecue or bonfire-night party. Spear a marshmallow onto a long skewer and toast near the glowing embers until slightly crispy on the outside and runny inside. Squash the marshmallow between two digestive biscuits – delicious!

# HER ROYAL HIGHNESS, THE PRINCESS OF WALES

## Royal Fudge

50g butter
4 tablespoons water
450g granulated sugar
1 397g can sweetened
  condensed milk

Put the butter, water and sugar into a large saucepan (preferably a non-stick saucepan). Put over a low heat and stir with a wooden spoon until the sugar is dissolved.

Add the condensed milk, turn up the heat and bring the mixture to the boil. Turn the heat down very low and simmer until the mixture thickens and turns a light brown colour – this should take between 20–30 minutes. Stir with a wooden spoon from time to time. Remove from the heat and beat well with a wooden spoon.

Take a knob of butter on a piece of kitchen paper and rub all round the inside of a 18 cm square tin. Pour the mixture into the tin. Leave to cool and set. Cut into squares when cold and lift the pieces of fudge carefully out with a palette knife.
*36 pieces*

# DRINKS

## CHRISTOPHER TIMOTHY
*Actor*

*Try this milkshake, it's wonderful!*

### Vet's Milkshake
**(Banana Milkshake)**

2 ripe bananas
2 level tablespoons soft
   brown sugar
300ml milk

Put the bananas into a medium sized bowl and mash up with a fork. Add the sugar and mash again. Slowly pour in the milk, and using a hand whisk, whisk the mixture for a minute or two. After twenty minutes standing in the fridge*, drink it all yourself.
*2 glasses*

*the *bowl* stands in the fridge, not you! CT

# JUNE WHITFIELD
*Actress*

## June's Cooler
**Home-made Lemonade**

You need an electric blender for this recipe. Make sure an adult helps you use it.

1 lemon (thin skinned are best)
2 tablespoons sugar
6 ice cubes
700ml cold water

Wash the lemon. Put it on to a board and using a sharp knife cut the lemon into quarters. Put the lemon, sugar, ice and water into the goblet. Secure the lid and turn on to a fast speed for 10 seconds. Holding a sieve over a wide necked jug strain the lemonade through it.

To serve, add 1 or 2 more ice cubes and float thin slices of extra lemon in the drink.

# GRAEME SOUNESS
*Footballer*

## Pop of the Kop
**(Party Punch)**

1 red skinned apple
1 orange
1 lemon
1 litre fresh orange juice
1 litre lemonade

Wash the fruit. Using a small sharp knife cut the apple into quarters and cut out the core. Cut into long slices and then across into small cubes. Thinly slice the orange and lemon. Put all the fruit into a large mixing bowl. Pour the orange juice over the fruit and top with lemonade. Then leave it for an hour to stand. Add a few ice cubes just before serving.
*about 12 glasses*

# ISLA ST CLAIR
*TV Presenter*

## Isla's Hot Chocolate

Make up a mug or cup of hot chocolate as directed on the packet and float two marshmallows on the top. They will melt and make a delicious creamy topping.

## Clair's Cool Coffee

Put 1–2 teaspoons liquid coffee essence into a glass. Three quarters fill the glass with cold milk and stir with a teaspoon. Top with a large dollop of vanilla or chocolate ice cream. Serve straightaway with a straw.

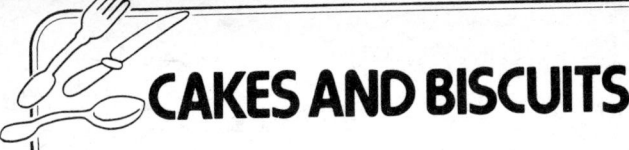

# CAKES AND BISCUITS

## BRIGIT FORSYTH
*Actress*

*These must be good because they always get eaten in one day!*

### Glamourjacks
**(Flapjacks)**

175g porridge oats
50g self-raising flour
50g dark soft brown sugar
100g butter or margarine
2 tablespoons golden syrup
vanilla essence

Put the oats, flour and sugar into a mixing bowl and rub together with your fingertips. Put the butter and syrup into a small saucepan and put over a medium heat. Stir with a wooden spoon until the butter has melted. Pour into the mixing bowl, add a few drops of vanilla essence and mix well together with a wooden spoon.

Take a small knob of butter on a piece of kitchen paper and rub the inside of a 28 × 20 cm shallow baking tin. Bake in a moderate oven (Gas No. 4 – 350°F – 180°C) for 25–30 minutes. Put the tin on to a board and leave for 10 minutes. Cut into slices but leave in the tin until cold.

*12 flapjacks*

# BILL BEAUMONT
*Former England Rugby Captain*
*TV Sports Presenter*

## Captain's Cake
### (Chocolate Cake)

75g plain cooking chocolate
200ml boiling water
175g butter or soft margarine
275g soft brown sugar
3 medium eggs
1 level teaspoon bicarbonate of soda
3 tablespoons milk
275g self-raising flour
pinch of salt

Break up the chocolate and put into a small bowl. Add the boiling water, stir and leave.

Put the margarine and sugar into a mixing bowl and sit the bowl on a damp cloth. Using a wooden spoon beat the mixture very hard until it is soft and fluffy. Holding an egg, tap it gently but firmly on the edge of the bowl and let it drop into the mixture. Beat it in well and repeat with the other eggs.

In a small bowl mix the bicarbonate of soda and milk together with a teaspoon. Sieve the flour and salt into the mixing bowl. Add the melted chocolate mixture and the dissolved bicarbonate. Using a tablespoon stir all the ingredients together.

Take a small knob of butter on a piece of kitchen paper and rub thoroughly all round the inside of a 24 cm round cake tin. Sprinkle a tablespoon of flour into the tin and shake it all round. Using a tablespoon put the cake mixture into the tin and spread it round with a palette knife.

Bake in a moderate oven (Gas No. 4 – 350°F – 180°C) for 1 hour. Leave for 10 minutes to cool in the tin and then turn it out and put it on a cooling wire.

Top with chocolate icing:
Sieve 8 tablespoons icing sugar and 1 tablespoon cocoa powder into a mixing bowl. Add 2–3 tablespoons boiling water and stir. The icing should be smooth, shiny and thick enough to be spread on the top of the cake.

# TIM BROOKE-TAYLOR
*Comic Actor*

## Goody Goody Yum Yums

50g margarine
50g soft brown sugar
1 dessertspoon golden syrup
40g plain flour

a pinch ginger
25g flaked almonds
6 glacé cherries – chopped
100g plain cooking chocolate

Put the margarine, sugar and syrup into a medium sized saucepan and put over a low heat to dissolve the sugar. Remove from the heat and using a wooden spoon beat in the flour, ginger, almonds and chopped cherries.

Cover a baking tray with greaseproof paper and rub a little butter on kitchen paper over the greaseproof paper. Using a teaspoon put small amounts of the mixture well apart on the greaseproof paper – about the size of marbles. Bake in a slow oven (Gas No. 2 – 300°F – 150°C) for ½ hour. Leave to set for about 2 minutes and then using a palette knife lift on to a cooling wire.

Regrease the paper with butter and cook more biscuits. Break the chocolate into small pieces into a small bowl. Quarter fill a small saucepan with water and bring to the boil. Remove from the heat and sit the bowl of chocolate over the hot water. When it has melted, use a palette knife to spread the flat underside of each biscuit with the chocolate.

*Approx 26 biscuits*

# STEVE OVETT
*Athlete*

## Cut-and-Run Cake

225g self-raising flour
pinch of salt
2 level teaspoons mixed spice
100g butter or margarine
100g castor sugar
225g mixed dried fruit
1 teaspoon finely grated lemon rind
1 medium egg
a little milk

Sieve the flour, salt and spice into a large mixing bowl. Cut the butter into small pieces and drop into the flour. Using your fingertips rub the butter into the flour quickly and lightly, until the mixture looks like fine breadcrumbs. Add the sugar, fruit and lemon rind, rub in and make a hole in the centre.

Tap the middle of the egg shell on the side of a measuring jug and let the egg drop into the jug. Whisk up with a fork and make up to 150ml with milk. Pour this into the flour and using a wooden spoon beat the mixture. Take a knob of butter on a piece of kitchen paper and rub the inside of a 15 cm round cake tin. Put in the mixture and spread round with a palette knife. Bake in a moderate oven (Gas No. 4 – 350°F – 180°C) for 1¼–1½ hours until golden. Turn out and cool on a wire tray.

# BRYAN MOSLEY
*Actor*

*Hey up and good luck!*

## Grocer's Goo Cake

100g digestive biscuits
100g walnuts
50g glacé cherries
100g marshmallows
50g butter
1 196g can condensed milk
50g oats

Put the biscuits into a polythene bag and crush them with a rolling pin. Tip them into a mixing bowl.

Using a small sharp knife cut the walnuts and cherries roughly into quarters. Add the nuts, cherries and marshmallows to the bowl.

Put the butter and condensed milk into a small saucepan and put over a very low heat to melt the butter. Pour this into the dry ingredients and mix together with a wooden spoon.

Cut a piece of foil approximately 25 × 18 cms and sprinkle oats over this. The mixture is very 'gooey' at this stage but tip it on to the oats and shape it into a fat sausage, covered with the oats. Wrap the foil around the mixture securely and put it in a freezer for an hour.

Serve sliced and keep the goo cake, wrapped in the foil, in the refrigerator.

# HANNAH GORDON
*Actress*

*This loaf is very easy and very good, especially when cut into thick slices and buttered.*

## Malt Loaf

Use a teacup to measure these ingredients:

2 cups self-raising flour
pinch of salt
1 cup dark soft brown sugar
1 cup mixed fruit – currants and raisins
1 cup milk
1 level tablespoon black treacle

Sieve the flour and salt into a mixing bowl. Add the sugar and fruit. Put the milk and treacle into a small saucepan and warm over a low heat. Pour the milk into the flour and beat well with a wooden spoon.

Take a knob of butter and rub all round the inside of a 20 × 13 × 8 cm loaf tin. Use a tablespoon to put in the mixture. Bake in a moderate oven (Gas No. 4 – 350°F – 180°C) for about 1 hour until golden brown. Leave in the tin for 5 minutes and then turn out on to a cooling wire.

Serve sliced and spread with butter.

# BARRY SHEENE
*World Champion Motorcycle Rider*

## Just Amazing Coffee Cake

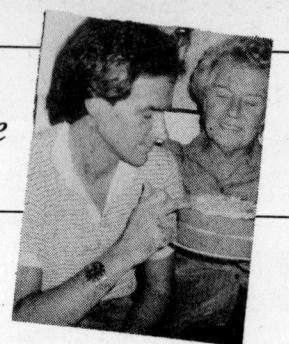

150g castor sugar
3 medium eggs
150g butter or margarine
1 tablespoon water
150g flour
50g chopped walnuts

**For filling and top:**
100g butter
150g icing sugar, sieved
few drops of coffee essence
few whole walnuts

Break the eggs into a mixing bowl and add the sugar. Whisk – an electric whisk is best – until the mixture is very thick, creamy and frothy (about 10 minutes). Put the water and butter into a small saucepan and heat gently to melt the butter. Pour this into the cake mixture and whisk it in. Sieve the flour and using a metal tablespoon fold in the flour and walnuts, very lightly and quickly.

Take a knob of butter on a piece of kitchen paper and rub all round the insides of two 18cm sandwich tins. Sprinkle a little flour into each. Divide the mixture between the tins and bake in a moderately hot oven (Gas No. 5 – 375°F – 190°C) for about 25–30 minutes, until the cakes are spongy when lightly pressed. Leave to cool for 5 minutes before turning out on to a cooling wire.

To make the icing, put the butter into a small bowl and beat it with a small wooden spoon. Add the sieved icing sugar slowly and beat it in. Add a few drops of coffee essence.

When the cakes are cold, using a knife spread half the icing on one cake and place the other cake on top. Spread the remaining icing on the top and decorate with a few walnuts.

# LAWRIE McMENEMY
*Southampton Football Club Manager*

*Happy Eating!*

## Manager's Majorcan Slice

100g butter or soft margarine
100g castor sugar
2 large eggs
100g currants
50g glacé cherries – chopped
110g ground almonds
50g self-raising flour

Put the margarine and sugar into a mixing bowl and sit this on a damp cloth. Using a wooden spoon beat the mixture hard until it is soft, light and fluffy. Carefully tap the middle of the egg shell on the side of the bowl, letting the egg drop into the mixture. Beat it in and repeat with the second egg. Add the currants, chopped cherries and ground almond. Sieve in the self-raising flour and using a tablespoon stir the mixture thoroughly.

Take a knob of butter on a piece of kitchen paper and rub it round the inside of a 18 cm square cake tin. Bake in a moderate oven (Gas No. 3 – 325°F – 160°C) for about 1 hour until it is a light golden brown. Leave in the tin for a few minutes to cool and then turn it out on to a cooling wire. When cold, cut into 16 squares.

# STUART HALL
*TV Presenter*

## Knock-out Krispies
**(Crispy Cereal Cakes)**

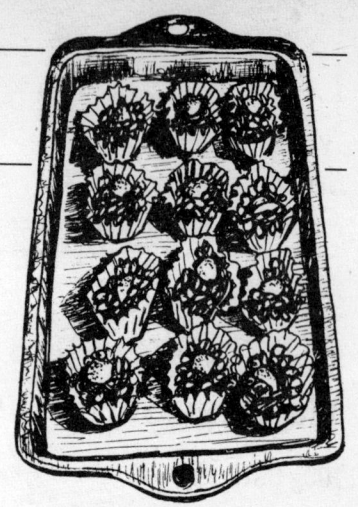

50g plain cooking chocolate
6 glacé cherries
25g chopped nuts – walnuts or hazelnuts
3–4 handfuls Rice Krispies

Half fill a medium sized saucepan with water and bring to the boil. Break the chocolate into a mixing bowl. Remove the saucepan from the heat and sit the bowl of chocolate on top of the pan.

Using a small sharp knife cut the cherries into quarters. When the chocolate has melted add the nuts, Rice Krispies and half the cherries to the bowl. Stir with a tablespoon to make sure everything is coated with chocolate.

Put 12 paper cases on to a baking tray and divide the mixture between them. Place a piece of cherry on top of each one. Leave the tray in the refrigerator until set – about half an hour.
*12 cakes*

# FLOELLA BENJAMIN
*Children's TV Presenter*

*This recipe is easy to make and looks most effective*

## Wally Cake

284ml double cream
2 teaspoons instant coffee
1 packet of 16 sponge finger
   biscuits
a few nuts and glacé cherries
   to decorate

Whisk the cream until thick and fluffy. Put the coffee into a cup and add a little very hot water. Stir with a teaspoon and fill up the cup with cold water. Dip each end of four sponge fingers quickly into the coffee – do not let them get too soggy! Lay them on a plate and using a knife spread some of the cream over them. Layer up the 'coffee fingers' and cream – finishing with the cream. Sprinkle a few nuts over the top and add a few cherries. Put in the refrigerator and serve very cold.
*4 servings*

This recipe is even more delicious if freshly ground coffee is made up, strained and used for dipping the fingers in.

# JANET BROWN
*Impressionist*

## Brown's American Brownies

25g walnuts
100g self-raising flour
pinch of salt
50g margarine
100g castor sugar
2 tablespoons water
150g plain cooking chocolate
 – broken into pieces
2 medium eggs
vanilla essence

Put the walnuts into a mixing bowl and break into small pieces by pressing them with a wooden spoon. Sieve in the flour and salt.

Put the margarine, sugar and water into a medium sized saucepan and bring to the boil. Stir with a wooden spoon all the time to dissolve the sugar. Remove from the heat and add the chocolate and stir until melted. Add the eggs one at a time and beat after adding each one until the mixture is smooth and shiny. Beat in the flour and nuts.

Take a knob of butter on a piece of kitchen paper and rub all round the inside of a 20 cm shallow square baking tin. Bake in a moderate oven (Gas No. 3 – 325°F – 160°C) for 30–35 minutes. Put the tin on to a board until cold and then cut into squares.
*16 brownies*

Keep in an airtight tin.

# PAUL DANIELS
*Magician*

## Magic Biscuits

1 rounded tablespoon golden syrup
140g butter
100g castor sugar
120g plain flour
2 level teaspoons bicarbonate of soda
75g rolled oats
50g dessicated coconut

Put the syrup, butter and sugar into a small saucepan and put over a low heat to melt and dissolve the sugar. Put the remaining ingredients into a mixing bowl.

Pour the butter mixture into the dry ingredients in the bowl and stir well with a wooden spoon. Leave the mixture to cool for about 15 minutes.

Take a little butter on a piece of kitchen paper and rub over 2 baking trays. Using your hands roll a little of the mixture – about the size of a marble – and put it on the baking trays. Spread the 'marbles' out as they will spread during cooking.

Bake in a moderate oven (Gas No. 3 – 325°F – 160°C) for 15 minutes until they are golden brown. Leave for a few minutes on the tray and then using a palette knife, lift the biscuits on to a cooling wire.

Now bake another batch of biscuits.

*Approx. 60 biscuits*

# PAUL & LINDA McCARTNEY
*Singers*

## Wings Special
**(Victoria Sponge Cake)**

100g soft margarine
100g castor sugar
2 medium eggs
100g self-raising flour
apricot jam (or your favourite flavour)
a little icing sugar

Take a knob of butter on a piece of kitchen paper and rub all round the insides of two 18 cm sandwich tins. Add a teaspoon of flour to each tin and shake so that the flour sticks to the butter.

Put the margarine and castor sugar into a large mixing bowl. Sit the bowl on a damp cloth and using a wooden spoon beat the mixture hard until it is soft and creamy. Tap the middle of the egg on the edge of the bowl and pull apart the shell halves so the egg drops into the mixture. Beat hard, add the second egg and beat again. Sieve the flour into the bowl and stir it in.

Divide the mixture evenly between the two tins and spread round lightly with a palette knife. Bake in a moderately hot oven (Gas No. 5 – 375°F – 190°C) for about 25 minutes. Leave in the tins for a few minutes before carefully turning out onto a cooling wire.

When they are cold spread one half with jam and put the other half on top. Sieve a little icing sugar over the cake and serve on a plate.

# PUDDINGS

## JULIA WILLIAMS
*Actress*

### Angels' Orange Surprise

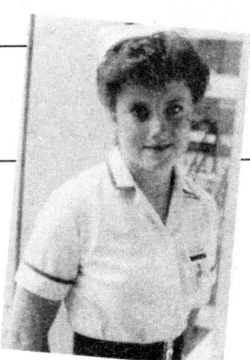

4 medium sized oranges
a little vanilla ice cream
2 egg whites (see how to separate egg whites on p. 76)
100g castor sugar

Wash the oranges and using a small sharp knife cut off the tops – you want the oranges to stand up, so leave the flattest end for the base. Use a grapefruit knife to carefully cut out the flesh – taking care not to cut through the skin. Put the flesh into a small bowl and roughly chop up.

Put the oranges on to an ovenproof plate or tin and put a spoonful of ice cream into each. Put in the orange flesh on top.

Using a hand whisk, whisk the egg whites in a mixing bowl until they are very stiff and frothy. Carefully and quickly fold in the castor sugar with a metal tablespoon – take great care *not* to stir.

Divide the meringue between the tops of the 4 oranges. Bake in a very hot oven (Gas No. 8 – 450°F – 230°C) for 5 minutes until the meringue is golden. Serve immediately!

*4 servings*

# DAVID JENSEN
*Disc Jockey*

*This is my ideal dessert!*

## Kid's Mousse
**(Chocolate Mousse)**

100g plain chocolate
50g castor sugar
3 medium eggs
1–2 teaspoons coffee essence
2 tablespoons cream

Break the chocolate up into a mixing bowl and add the sugar. Put a little water into a medium sized saucepan and bring to the boil. Place the mixing bowl on to the saucepan and turn the heat down to very low.

Holding an egg in one hand, tap the middle of the shell on to the edge of another mixing bowl. Carefully let the egg white fall into the bowl while keeping the yolk in the shell. Tip the yolk from one half shell to the other. Repeat with the other eggs.

When the chocolate has melted add the egg yolks, coffee and cream and whisk together. Using a clean whisk, whisk the egg whites until they are very stiff and frothy.

Remove the bowl of chocolate mixture from the saucepan of hot water and put on a board. Using a metal tablespoon lift the beaten egg white into the chocolate mixture. Very carefully fold the egg white into the chocolate. Do not stir, simply lift the chocolate and fold it into the egg whites.

Quickly and lightly divide the mixture between 4 glass dishes and put into the refrigerator to set. This will take about 1 hour.

*4 servings*

# RUSS ABBOT
*Comedian*

*I love this sweet with custard, as cooked by my wife Tricia.*

## Madhouse Gooseberry Tart

200g self-raising or plain flour
pinch of salt
50g lard
50g margarine
a little cold water
1 383g can gooseberry pie filling

Sieve the flour and salt into a mixing bowl. Using a small sharp knife cut up the lard and margarine and drop into the flour. Using only your fingertips, gently lift up and rub the fat into the flour until the mixture looks like fine breadcrumbs or sand. Add a little water (3–4 tablespoons) and stir into the flour with a palette knife to make a firm dough.

Sprinkle a little flour on to the worktop and rolling pin. Gently and lightly roll the pastry into a circle, until the pastry is .5 cms thick. Lift the pastry on to a 22 cms ovenproof plate and trim off the edges with a sharp knife.

Open the can of pie filling and spread over the flat part of the pastry. Collect the scraps of pastry together and roll out again into an oblong. Cut long, 1 cm wide strips of pastry and twist each one. Damp the edge of the pie and lay the twisted strips over the gooseberries to form a nice pattern. Press the ends on to the damp pie edge. Bake in a hot oven (Gas No. 6 – 400°F – 200°C) for 25–30 minutes until the pastry is a light golden brown. Can be served hot or cold.
*6 servings*

# TODD CARTY
*Actor*

## Tucker's Apple Amber

900g cooking apples
100g granulated sugar
rind and juice of 1 lemon
50g butter
2 medium eggs
100g castor sugar

Using a small sharp knife cut the apples into quarters, remove the core and peel. Slice the apples thinly and put into a medium sized saucepan with the granulated sugar, lemon rind and juice and the butter. Put over a moderate heat and cook for 8–10 minutes, until the apples are tender. Stir with a wooden spoon from time to time. Remove from the heat and beat the apples with a fork.

Take an egg and tap the middle of it on the edge of a clean mixing bowl. Holding the egg over the bowl carefully pull apart the shell and let the egg white fall into the bowl while keeping the yolk in the shell. Tip the yolk from one half to the other until all the white has fallen into the bowl. Beat the yolk into the apple mixture and then repeat with the other egg. Pour the apple mixture into an ovenproof dish.

Using a hand whisk, whisk the egg whites until they are very thick and fluffy. Using a metal tablespoon quickly and lightly fold in the castor sugar. Do not stir, just lift the egg whites through the sugar. Pile on top of the apple mixture and gently push the meringue to the edges with a fork. Rough up the meringue a little. Bake in a moderate oven (Gas No. 3 – 325°F – 160°C) for about 45 minutes, until the meringue is a light golden brown.
*4 servings*

# IAN OGILVY
*Actor*

## Saint Sauce
**(Hot Chocolate Sauce)**

4 tablespoons milk
2 68g Mars Bars

To serve with ice cream

Put the milk into a small saucepan. Using a small sharp knife cut each Mars Bar into 6 pieces and add these to the milk. Put the saucepan on to a very low heat and stir the sauce with a small wooden spoon until the Mars Bars have melted. Pour over ice cream and serve straightaway.
*4 servings*

# STEPHANIE TURNER
*Actress*

*This recipe is very rich, very delicious and very easy to make!*

## Bravo Macaroons
**(Macaroon Creams)**

1 macaroon biscuit
125ml double cream
1 egg white (see how to separate eggs on p. 76)
1 dessertspoon castor sugar

By hand, crumble the macaroon biscuit on to a plate. Using a hand whisk, whisk the cream in a medium sized bowl until thick and fluffy.

Using a clean whisk, whisk the egg white in a small bowl until it is stiff. Using a tablespoon lightly fold the sugar into the egg white.

Add all the ingredients to the cream and lightly fold in with a tablespoon. Divide between 4 glasses or bowls and leave in the refrigerator for an hour before serving.
*4 servings*

# PAULA ANN BLAND
*Actress*

## Grange Hill Gateau
### (Black Forest Gateau)

1 frozen chocolate fresh cream sponge
1 450g can pitted black cherries
2 tablespoons instant chocolate sauce
150ml double cream
20g plain chocolate – grated

Take the cake while it is still frozen and put it on a board. Using a large sharp knife cut the cake across in half through the cream in the centre. Put one half on to a plate. Open the can of cherries and drain the juice into a jug. Cover the bottom half of the sponge with cherries, leaving a few to decorate the top later on. Trail the chocolate sauce over the cherries and cover with the top half of the sponge. Pour the cream into a small bowl and using a hand whisk, whisk the cream until it is thick and fluffy. Using a palette knife spread the cream over the top and sides of the cake. Leave the cake to defrost at room temperature (about 2 hours). Just before serving decorate the top with the grated chocolate and the remaining cherries.
*6 servings*

You could use the cherry juice later on to make up a jelly or a milkshake.

# BOB WILSON
*TV Sports Presenter*

## Match of the Day Cheesecake
### (St Clements Cheesecake)

200g digestive biscuits
25g butter or margarine
1 rounded tablespoon golden syrup
2 teaspoons cocoa powder
450g cottage cheese
1 lemon } finely grated
2 oranges } rind and juice
18g or 6 level teaspoons gelatine
100g castor sugar
300ml double cream – whipped until thick and fluffy

Decorate if you like with
Grated chocolate
Slices of orange – fresh or jellied orange slices

Put the biscuits into a polythene bag and crush with a rolling pin. Put the butter, syrup and cocoa into a saucepan and melt over a low heat. Remove from the heat and, using a wooden spoon, mix in the biscuit crumbs. Tip into a 25 cm loose bottomed tin with a spring clip and spread over the base.

Using a wooden spoon press the cheese through a sieve into a mixing bowl. Add the orange and lemon rind to this. Pour the orange and lemon juice into a measuring jug and make up to 300ml with water. Quarter fill a medium sized saucepan with water and bring to the boil. Remove the saucepan from the heat and sit the measuring jug in the hot water. Sprinkle the gelatine into the jug and stir with a tablespoon until dissolved.

Add the castor sugar and stir again until dissolved. Pour

the liquid into the cheese and stir well. Using a tablespoon gently stir in the whipped cream – the mixture is runny at this stage. Pour this into the tin on top of the biscuit base. Leave to set – this will take about 2 hours but leave it overnight if you can.

Undo the tin carefully but leave the cheesecake on the base. Decorate with grated chocolate and orange slices.

# ERNIE WISE
*Comedian*

*My recipe is definitely banned for all those people on diets, but it helps to keep my short, fat, hairy legs in fine fettle – Ernie.*

## Wisecrack Crunch
**(Blackberry & Apple Crunch)**

450g cooking apples
1 × 220g can blackberries
4 tablespoons golden syrup
50g margarine
2 teacups cornflakes

Using a small sharp knife cut the apples into quarters, cut out the core and peel off the skin. Thinly slice the apples and put into a 1 litre ovenproof dish. Open the can of blackberries and tip the fruit and juice over the apples.

Trail 2 tablespoons of the syrup over the fruit. Bake in a moderate oven (Gas No. 4 – 350°F – 180°C) for 20 minutes.

Put the other 2 tablespoons of syrup and the margarine into a small saucepan. Put over a low heat to melt the margarine. Remove from the heat and stir in the cornflakes with a tablespoon.

Remove the dish of fruit from the oven and spoon the cornflake mixture on the top. Return to the oven for 25–30 minutes until the topping is crisp and golden.

*4–6 servings*

# SARAH LAM
*Actress*

## Bread and Butter Pudding

butter to spread
8–10 slices bread
50g raisins
50g sultanas
500ml milk
a few drops vanilla essence
pinch of salt
25g castor sugar

Spread butter on each slice of bread. Put 5 slices onto a board and cover with the raisins and sultanas. Cover with the other slices to make sandwiches. Cut each one with a large sharp knife into quarters. Arrange them into an ovenproof dish. Mix the milk, vanilla and salt in a jug and pour over the bread. Sprinkle with sugar. Leave for 1 hour. Bake in moderately hot oven (Gas No. 5 – 375°F – 190°C) for about 45 minutes until the top is golden brown.
*5–6 servings*

# MICK ROBERTSON
*TV Presenter*

## Freetime Chocolate Bananas

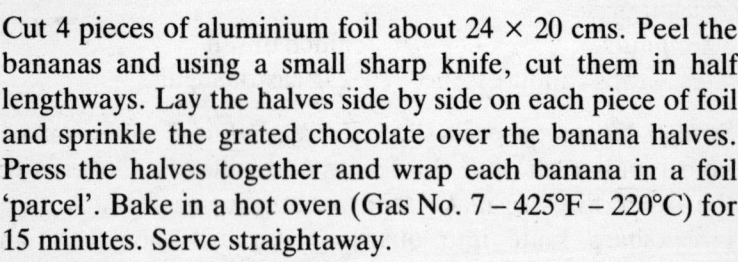

4 bananas
50g plain or milk chocolate – grated

Cut 4 pieces of aluminium foil about 24 × 20 cms. Peel the bananas and using a small sharp knife, cut them in half lengthways. Lay the halves side by side on each piece of foil and sprinkle the grated chocolate over the banana halves. Press the halves together and wrap each banana in a foil 'parcel'. Bake in a hot oven (Gas No. 7 – 425°F – 220°C) for 15 minutes. Serve straightaway.
*4 servings*

These are extra delicious if spread with whipped double cream after cooking. They may be cooked in the hot embers of a barbecue or bonfire for about 10 minutes.

# JON PERTWEE
*Actor*

## Worzel's Fresh Fruit Salad

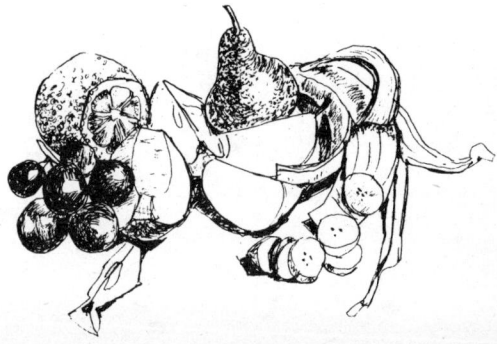

100g sugar
300ml water
1 lemon
2 bananas
2 eating apples – red-skinned look nice
1 pear
a few black grapes

Put the sugar and water into a small saucepan and put over a low heat. Stir once and then simmer for 5 minutes. Squeeze the juice from the lemon and pour into a serving bowl.

Peel the bananas and using a small sharp knife cut them into thin slices. Wash the apples and pear, cut into quarters and cut out the core. Cut the quarters into 1 cm thick long slices and then cut again into small cubes. Add the cut fruit to the bananas and toss in the lemon juice.

Wash the grapes, cut in half and pick out the pips. Add to the bowl and pour the syrup over the fruit. Put the fruit into the refrigerator for 1 hour before serving.

*4 servings*

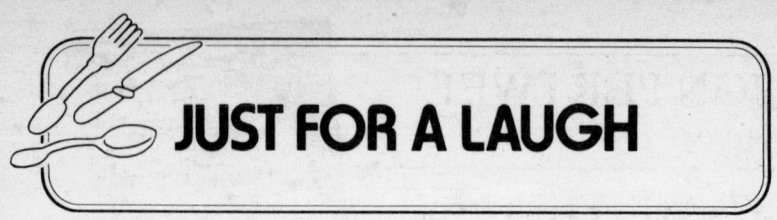

# JUST FOR A LAUGH

## BARRY CRYER
*Scriptwriter and Comedian*

### Hard-Boiled Egg

Take one egg (brown or white – brown for extra richness). Place in a pan of cold water. (Aluminium for preference – the pan not the water). Boil the water. Upon the first bubble, start the egg timer. When the sand has fully descended, add a count of 35 and then remove the egg with a tablespoon. Place in the egg cup, top downwards. Slice with a knife, or, if a runnier consistency is desired, strike with the egg spoon. Add salt with the finger. Eat.

# MARTI CAINE
*Comedienne*

## Beans on Toast

Take one tin of beans, open. Take 11 slices of bread, toast until you get two that still look reasonably like bread. Discard black charred bits. Empty beans into a pan and heat. Put warm beans onto buttered toast, plunge smoking pan into cold water immediately. By this time the beans are beginning to coagulate, but a sharp burst in the microwave helps.

# JOHN CLEESE
*Comic Actor*

## Ferret Supreme

First of all you want a fresh ferret. To make sure the ferret is fresh hold it and twist it firmly. If the ferret is fresh it will make a lot of noise. Then you want to drop it into a vat of boiling calves foot jelly for two days and then take it and simmer very gently in the Bay of Biscay. Then allow to cool and serve with grated motor cycle and grey sports jacket.

*This is what the press said about my ferret recipe: 'I have never tasted food like it before'* – **Observer**

# JOHNNY MORRIS
*TV Naturalist*

## Garden Peas

Buy a packet of garden peas called Duke of Albany. Plant them, watch them grow and talk to them. When ready, pick them and shell them at once and simmer until ready. Lock all doors, take phone off the hook, turn off the radio. Turn peas onto a warm plate and apply white pepper. Eat in silence and be thankful that they are not frozen peas.

# KIERAN PRENDIVILLE
*TV Presenter*

## Lettuce

My favourite dish is 'Big Mac' hamburger, without the bun, the meat, the dressing, the onions and the tomato sauce. You see, I quite like lettuce.

# CHAS AND DAVE
*Singers*

## Stuffed Camel

1 medium camel
20 rabbits (stewed)
40 kilos of tomatoes
4 lambs
150 eggs (boiled)
salt and seasonings

Stuff eggs into tomatoes. Stuff tomatoes into rabbits. Stuff rabbits into lambs. Stuff lambs into camel. Roast until tender.
*Serves 150 people*

# SPIKE MILLIGAN
*Comedian*

*Believe me, spaghetti as a sweet is delicious.*

## Sweet Spaghetti

You cook the spaghetti (without salt) for about fifteen minutes and while it is cooking whip up a carton of double cream and then add castor sugar. Serve this mixture on top of the hot spaghetti.